Principal Speech Against Unconditional Repeal

WILLIAM JENNINGS BRYAN

1893

TABLE OF CONTENTS

PRINCIPAL SPEECH AGAINST UNCONDITIONAL REPEAL

Mr. Speaker: I shall accomplish my full purpose if I am able to impress upon the members of the House the far-reaching consequences which may follow our action and quicken their appreciation of the grave responsibility which presses upon us. Historians tell us that the victory of Charles Martel at Tours determined the history of all Europe for centuries. It was a contest "between the Crescent and the Cross," and when, on that fateful day, the Frankish prince drove back the followers of Abderrahman he rescued the West from "the all-destroying grasp of Islam," and saved to Europe its Christian civilization. A greater than Tours is here! In my humble judgment the vote of this House on the subject under consideration may bring to the people of the West and South, to the people of the United States, and to all mankind, weal or woe beyond the power of language to describe or imagination to conceive.

In the princely palace and in the humblest hamlet; by the financier and by the poorest toiler; here, in Europe and everywhere, the proceedings of this Congress, upon this problem will be read and studied; and as our actions bless or blight we shall be commended or condemned. The President of the United States, in the discharge of his duty as he sees it, has sent to Congress a message calling attention to the present financial situation, and recommending the unconditional repeal of the Sherman law as the only means of securing immediate relief. Some outside of this hall have insisted that the President's recommendation imposes upon Democratic members an obligation, as it were, to carry out his wishes, and over-zealous friends have even suggested that opposition to his views might subject the hardy dissenter to administrative displeasure. They do the President great injustice who presume that he would forget for a moment the independence of the two branches of Congress. He would not be worthy of our admiration or even respect if he demanded a homage which would violate the primary principles of free representative government.

Let his own language rebuke those who would disregard their pledges to their own people in order to display a false fealty. In the message which he sent to Congress in December, 1885, he said, in words which may well be our guide in this great crisis: "The zealous watchfulness of our constituencies, great and small, supplements their suffrages, and before the tribunal they establish every public servant should be judged." Among the many grand truths expressed felicitously by the President during his public career none show a truer conception of official duty or describe with more clearness the body from which the member receives his authority and to which he owes his responsibility.

Yes, Mr. Speaker, it is before the tribunal established by our constituencies, and before that tribunal only that we must appear for judgment upon our actions here. When we each accepted a commission from 180,000 people we pledged ourselves to protect their rights from invasion and to reflect their wishes to the best of our ability, and we must stand defenseless beore the bar if our only excuse is "he recommended it." And remember, sir, that these constituencies include not bankers, brokers, and boards of trade only, but embrace people in every station and condition of life; and in that great court from whose decision there is no appeal every voter has an equal voice. That the Democratic party understands the duty of the Representative, is evident from the fact that it found it necessary to nonconcur in a similar recommendation made by the President in 1885.

In the message which he sent to the Forty-ninth Congress, at the beginning of the first session, we find these words:

Prosperity hesitates upon our threshold because of the dangers and uncertainties surrounding this question. Capital timidly shrinks from trade, and investors are unwilling to take the chance of the questionable shape in which their money will be returned to them, while enterprise halts at a risk against which care and sagacious management do not protect.

As a necessary consequence, labor lacks employment, and suffering and distress are visited upon a portion of our fellow-citizens especially entitled to the careful consideration of those charged with the duties of legislation. No interest appeals to us so strongly for a safe and stable currency as the vast army of the unemployed. I recommend the suspension of the compulsory coinage of silver dollars, directed by the law passed in February, 1878.

It will be seen that the same forces were at work then as now; the same apprehensions existed as now; the same pressure was brought from the same sources in favor of the debasement of silver; but the members of Congress, refusing to take counsel of their fears, stood by the record of both great parties and by the Nation's history and retained the coinage of silver as then provided for. Let it be said to the credit of the Democratic party that in the House only thirty-three of its members voted to suspend the Bland law, while 130 are recorded against suspension. Time has proved that the members, reflecting the opinions of their people, were wiser than the Executive, and he is doubtless grateful today that they did not follow his suggestion.

I have read with care the message sent to us last week, and have considered it in the light of every reasonable construction of which it is capable. If I am able to understand its language it points to the burial of silver, with no promise of resurrection. Its reasoning is in the direction of a single standard. It leads irresistibly to universal gold monometallism—to a realm over whose door is written: "Abandon hope, all ye who enter here!" Before that door I stop, appalled. Have gentlemen considered the effect of a single gold standard universally adopted? Let us not deceive ourselves with the hope that we can discard silver for gold, and that other nations will take it up and keep it as a part of the world's currency. When all the silver available for coinage could gain admission to some mints and all the gold available for coinage would find a place for mintage, and some nation like France maintained the parity by means of bimetallism it was of comparatively little importance whether a particular nation used silver, or gold, or both.

Exchange did not fluctuate and trade could be carried on without inconvenience. But times have changed. One nation after another has closed its mints to silver until the white metal has, in European countries, been made an outcast by legislation and has shown a bullion value different from its coinage value. India, at last, guided by the misrepresentations of the metropolitan press, which proclaimed as certain what was never probable, has suspended free coinage, fearing that this country would stop the purchase of silver. If the United States, the greatest silver producing nation, which now utilizes more than one-third of the total annual product of the world, closes its mint to the coinage of silver, what assurance have we that it can retain its place as primary money in the commercial world?

Is it not more reasonable to suppose that a further fall in the bullion value of silver will be followed by a demand for a limitation of the legal tender qualities of the silver already in existence? That is already being urged by some. Is it not reasonable to suppose that our hostile action will lead to hostile action on the part of other nations? Every country must have money for its people, and if silver is abandoned and gold substituted it must be drawn from the world's already scanty supply. We hear much about a "stable currency" and an "honest dollar." It is a significant fact that those who have spoken in favor of unconditional repeal have for the most part

7

avoided a discussion of the effect of an appreciating standard. They take it for granted that a gold standard is not only an honest standard, but the only stable standard. I denounce that child of ignorance and avarice, the gold dollar under a universal gold standard, as the most dishonest dollar which we could employ.

I stand upon the authority of every intelligent writer upon political economy when I assert that there is not and never has been an honest dollar. An honest dollar is a dollar absolutely stable in relation to all other things. Laughlin, in his work on Bimetallism, says:

Monometallists do not—as is often said—believe that gold remains absolutely stable in value. They hold that there is no such thing as a "standard of value" for future payments in either gold or silver which remains absolutely invariable.

He even suggests a multiple standard for long-time contracts. I quote his words:

As regards National debts, it is distinctly averred that neither gold nor silver forms a just measure of deferred payments, and that if justice in long contracts is sought for, we should not seek it by the doubtful and untried expedient of international bimetallism, but by the clear and certain method of a multiple standard, a unit based upon the selling prices of a number of articles of general consumption. A long-time contract would thereby be paid at its maturity by the same purchasing power as was given in the beginning.

Jevons, one of the most generally accepted of the writers in favor of a gold standard, admits the instability of a single standard, and in language very similar to that above quoted suggests the multiple standard as the most equitable if practicable. Chevalier, who wrote a book in 1858 to show the injustice of allowing a debtor to pay his debts in a cheap gold dollar, recognized the same fact, and said:

If the value of the metal declined, the creditor would suffer a loss upon the quantity he had received, if, on the contrary, it rose, the debtor would have to pay more than he calculated upon.

I am on sound and scientific ground, therefore, when I say that a dollar approaches honesty as its purchasing power approaches stability. If I borrow a thousand dollars today and next year pay the debt with a thousand dollars which will secure exactly as much of all things desirable as the one thousand which I borrowed, I have paid in honest dollars. If the money has increased or decreased in purchasing power, I have satisfied my debt with dishonest dollars. While the Government can say that a given weight of gold or silver shall constitute a dollar, and invest that dollar with legal-tender qualities, it cannot fix the purchasing power of the dollar. That must depend upon the law of supply and demand, and it may be well to suggest that this Government never tried to fix the exchangeable value of a dollar until it began to limit the number of dollars coined.

If the number of dollars increases more rapidly than the need for dollars—as it did after the gold discoveries of 1849—the exchangeable value of each dollar will fall and prices rise. If the demand for dollars increases faster than the number of dollars—as it did after 1800—the price of each dollar will rise and prices generally will fall. The relative value of the dollar may be changed by natural causes or by legislation. An increased supply—the demand remaining the same—or a decreased demand—the supply remaining the same—will reduce the exchangeable value of each dollar. Natural causes may act on both supply and demand; as, for instance, by increasing the product from the mines or by increasing the amount consumed in the arts. Legislation acts directly on the demand, and thus affects the price, since the demand is one of the factors in fixing the price.

If by legislative action the demand for silver is destroyed and the demand for gold is increased by making it the only standard, the exchangeable value of each unit of that standard, or dollar, as we call it, will be increased. If the exchangeable value of the dollar is increased by legislation the debt of the debtor is increased, to his injury and to the advantage of the creditor. And let me suggest here, in reply to the gentleman from Massachusetts (Mr. McCall), who said that the money loaner was entitled to the advantages derived from improved machinery and inventive genius, that he is mistaken. The laboring man and the producer are entitled to these benefits, and the money loaner, by every law of justice, ought to be content with a dollar equal in purchasing power to the dollar which he loaned, and any one desiring more than that desires a dishonest dollar, it matters not what name he may give to it. Take an illustration: John Doe, of Nebraska, has a farm worth $2,000 and mortgages it to Richard Roe, of Massachusetts, for $1,000. Suppose the value of the monetary unit is increased by legislation which creates a greater demand for gold. The debt is increased. If the increase amounts to 100 per cent. the Nebraska farmer finds that the prices of his products have fallen one-half and his land loses one-half its value, unless the price is maintained by the increased population incident to a new country.

The mortgage remains nominally the same, though the debt has actually become twice as great. Will he be deceived by the cry of "honest dollar?" If he should loan a Nebraska neighbor a hog weighing 100 pounds and the next spring demand in return a hog weighing 200 pounds he would be called dishonest, even though he contended that he was only demanding one hog—just the number he loaned. Society has become accustomed to some very nice distinctions. The poor man is called a socialist if he believes that the wealth of the rich should be divided among the poor, but the rich man is called a financier if he devises a plan by which the pittance of the poor can be converted to his use.

The poor man who takes property by force is called a thief, but the creditor who can by legislation make a debtor pay a dollar twice as large as he borrowed is lauded as the friend of a sound currency. The man who wants the people to destroy the Government is an anarchist, but the man who wants the Government to destroy the people is a patriot.

The great desire now seems to be to restore confidence, and some have an idea that the only way to restore confidence is to coax the money loaner to let go of his hoard by making the profits too tempting to be resisted. Capital is represented as a shy and timid maiden who must be courted, if won. Let me suggest a plan for bringing money from Europe. If it be possible, let us enact a law "Whereas confidence must be restored; and whereas money will always come from its hiding place if the inducement is sufficient, Therefore, be it enacted, That every man who borrows $1 shall pay back $2 and interest (the usury law not to be enforced)."

Would not English capital come "on the swiftest ocean greyhounds?" The money loaner of London would say: "I will not loan in India or Egypt or in South America. The inhabitants of those countries are a wicked and ungodly people and refuse to pay more than they borrowed. I will loan in the United States, for there lives an honest people, who delight in a sound currency and pay in an honest dollar." Why does not some one propose that plan? Because no one would dare to increase by law the number of dollars which the debtor must pay, and yet by some it is called wise statesmanship to do indirectly and in the dark what no man has the temerity to propose directly and openly.

We have been called cranks and lunatics and idiots because we have warned our fellow-men against the inevitable and intolerable consequences which would follow the adoption of a gold standard by all the world. But who, I ask, can be silent in the presence of such impending calamities? The United States, England, France, and Germany own today about $2,600,000,000 of the world's supply of gold coin, or about five-sevenths of the total amount, and yet these four nations contain but a small fraction of the inhabitants of the globe. What will be the exchangeable value of a gold dollar when India's people, outnumbering alone the inhabitants of the four great nations named, reach out after their share of gold coin? What will be the final price of gold when all the nations of the Occident and Orient join in the scramble?

A distinguished advocate of the gold standard said recently, in substance: "Wheat has now reached a point where the English can aford to buy it, and gold will soon return to relieve our financial embarrassment." How delighted the farmer will be when he realizes what an opportunity he has to save his country! A nation in distress; banks failing; mines closed; laborers unemployed; enterprise at a standstill, and behold, the farmer, bowed with unceasing, even if unremunerative, toil, steps forth to save his country—by selling his wheat below the cost of production! And I am afraid he will even now be censured for allowing the panic to go as far as it has before reducing his prices.

It seems cruel that upon the growers of wheat and cotton, our staple exports, should be placed the burden of supplying us, at whatever cost, with the necessary gold, and yet the financier quoted has suggested the only means, except the issue of bonds, by which our stock of gold can be replenished. If it is difficult now to secure gold, what will be the condition when the demand is increased by its adoption as the world's only primary money? We would simply put gold upon an auction block, with every nation as a bidder, and each ounce of the standard metal would be knocked down to the one offering the most of all other kinds of property. Every disturbance of finance in one country would communicate itself to every other, and in the misery which would follow it would be of little consolation to know that others were suffering as much as, or more than, we.

I have only spoken of the immediate effects of the substitution of gold as the world's only money of ultimate redemption. The worst remains to be told. If, as in the resumption of specie payments in 1879, we could look forward to a time when the contraction would cease, the debtor might become a tenant upon his former estate and the home owner assume the role of the homeless with the sweet assurance that his children or his children's children might live to enjoy the blessings of a "stable currency." But, sir, the hapless and hopeless producer of wealth goes forth into a night illuminated by no star; he embarks upon a sea whose further shore no mariner may find; he travels in a desert where the ever-retreating mirage makes his disappointment a thousand-fold more keen. Let the world once commit its fortunes to the use of gold alone and it must depend upon the annual increase of that metal to keep pace with the need for money.

The Director of the Mint gives about $130,000,000 as the world's production last year. Something like one-third is produced in connection with silver, and must be lost if silver mining is rendered unproductive. It is estimated that nearly two-thirds of the annual product is used in the arts, and the amount so used is increasing. Where, then, is the supply to meet the increasing demands of an increasing population? Is there some new California or some undiscovered Australia yet to be explored?

Is it not probable that the supply available for coinage will diminish rather than increase? Jacobs, in his work on the Precious Metals, has calculated the appreciation of the monetary unit. He has shown that the almost imperceptible increase of 2 per cent. per year will amount to a total appreciation of 500 per cent. in a century. Or, to illustrate, that cotton at 10 cents today and wheat at 60 cents would mean cotton at 2 cents and wheat at 12 cents in one hundred years. A national, State or municipal debt renewed from time to time would, at the end of that period, be six times as great as when contracted, although several times the amount would have been paid in interest.

When one realizes the full significance of a constantly appreciating standard he can easily agree with Alison that the Dark Ages resulted from a failure of the money supply. How can anyone view with unconcern the attempt to turn back the tide of civilization by the complete debasement of one-half of the world's money! When I point to the distress which, not suddenly, but gradually is entering the habitations of our people; when I refer you to the census as conclusive evidence of the unequal distribution of wealth and of increasing tenancy among our people, of whom, in our cities, less than one-fourth now own their homes; when I suggest the possibility of this condition continuing until passed from a land of independent owners, we become a nation of landlords and tenants, you tremble for civil liberty itself. Free government cannot long survive when the thousands enjoy the wealth of the country and the million share its poverty in common. Even now you hear among the rich an occasionally expressed contempt for popular government, and among the poor a protest against legislation which makes them "toil that others may reap." I appeal to you to restore justice and bring back prosperity while yet a peaceable solution can be secured. We mourn the lot of unhappy Ireland, whose alien owners drain it of its home created wealth; but we may reach a condition, if present tendencies continue, when her position at this time will be an object of envy, and some poet may write of our cities as Goldsmith did of the "Deserted Village":

While scourged by famine from a smiling land,
The mournful peasant leads his humble band,
And, while he sinks without one hand to save,
The country blooms—a garden and a grave.

But, lest I may be accused of reasonless complaining, let me call unimpeachable witnesses who will testify to the truth of my premises and to the correctness of my conclusions.

Jevons says:

If all nations of the globe were suddenly and simultaneously to demonetize silver and require gold money a revolution in the value of gold would be inevitable.

Giffin, who is probably the most fanatical adherent of the gold standard, says, in his book entitled The Case Against Bimetallism:

The primary offender in the matter, perhaps, was Germany, which made a mistake, as I believe, in substituting gold for silver as the standard money of the country. ... To some extent also Italy has been an offender in this matter, the resumption of specie payments in that country on a gold basis being entirely a work of superfluity; the resumption on a silver basis would have been preferable. ... No doubt the pressure on gold would have been more severe than it has been if the United States had not passed the Bland coinage law.

The gentleman from Maryland (Mr. Rayner) said in the opening speech of this debate:

In my opinion there is not a sufficient amount of gold in existence to supply the demands of commerce and the necessities of the world's circulation.

Mr. Balfour, member of Parliament, in a speech recently made, said:

Let Germany, India, and the United States try a gold currency and a tremor seizes every one of our commercial magnates. They look forward, in the immediate future, to catastrophe, and feel that the ultimate result may be a slow appreciation of the standard of value, which is perhaps the most deadening and benumbing influence that can touch the enterprise of a nation.

Mr. Goschen, delegate from Great Britain, said at the International Monetary Conference in 1878:

If, however, other States were to carry on a propaganda in favor of a gold standard and the demonetization of silver, the Indian government would be obliged to reconsider its position and might be forced by events to take measures similar to those taken elsewhere. In that case the scramble to get rid of silver might provoke one of the gravest crises ever undergone by commerce. One or two States might demonetize silver without serious results, but if all demonetize there would be no buyers, and silver would fall in alarming proportions. ... If all States should resolve on the adoption of a gold standard, the question arose, would there be sufficient gold for the purpose without a tremendous crisis? There would be a fear on the one hand of a depreciation of silver, and one on the other of a rise in the value of gold, and a corresponding fall in the prices of all commodities.

Italy, Russia, and Austria, whenever they resume specie payments, would require metal, and if all other States went in the direction of a gold standard, these countries too would be forced to take gold. Resumption on their part would be facilitated by the maintenance of silver as a part of the legal tender of the world. The American proposal for a universal double standard seemed impossible of realization, a veritable Utopia; but the theory of a universal gold standard was Utopian, and indeed involved a false Utopia. It was better for the world at large that the two metals should continue in circulation than that one should be universally substituted for the other.

Thus does an eminent English monometallist denounce the idea of a universal gold standard and foretell its consequences. But we are not dependent for authority upon foreign advocates of a gold standard. Read the words of him who for many years was the guiding genius of the Republican party, Hon. James G. Blaine, and say whether he was a lunatic because he described in emphatic words the dangers attendant upon universal monometallism. He said upon the floor of the House, February 7, 1878:

On the much vexed and long mooted question as to a bimetallic or monometallic standard, my own views are sufficiently indicated in the remarks I have made. I believe the struggle now going on in this country and in other countries for a single gold standard would, if successful, produce widespread disaster in and throughout the commercial world.

The destruction of silver as money and establishing gold as the sole unit of value must have a ruinous effect on all forms of property except those investments which yield a fixed return in money. These would be enormously enhanced in value, and would gain a disproportionate and unfair advantage over every other species of property. If, as the most reliable statistics affirm, there are nearly $7,000,000,000 of coin or bullion in the world, not very unequally divided between gold and silver, it is impossible to strike silver out of existence as money without results which will prove distressing to millions and utterly disastrous to tons of thousands.

Again, he said:

I believe gold and silver coin to be the money of the Constitution; indeed, the money of the American people, anterior to the Constitution which the great organic law recognized as quite independent of its own existence. No power was conferred on Congress to declare either metal should not be money. Congress has, therefore, in my judgment, no power to demonetize silver any more than to demonetize gold.

Senator Sherman said in 1869:

The contraction of the currency is a far more distressing operation than Senators suppose. Our own and other nations have gone through that operation before. It is not possible to take that voyage without the sorest distress. To every person except a capitalist out of debt, or a salaried officer or annuitant, it is a period of loss, danger, lassitude of trade, fall of wages, suspension of enterprise, bankruptcy, and disaster. It means ruin of all dealers whose debts are twice their business capital, though one-third less than their actual property. It means the fall of all agricultural production without any great reduction of taxes. What prudent man would dare to build a house, a railroad, a factory, or a barn with this certain fact before him?

Let me quote from an apostle of the Democratic faith, whose distinguished services in behalf of his party and his country have won for him the esteem of all. Mr. Carlisle, then a member of the House of Representatives, said, February 21, 1878:

I know that the world's stock of precious metals is none too large, and I see no reason to apprehend that it will ever be so. Mankind will be fortunate indeed if the annual production of gold and silver coin shall keep pace with the annual increase of population, and industry. According to my views of the subject the conspiracy which seems to have been formed here and in Europe to destroy by legislation and otherwise from three-sevenths to one-half the metallic money of the world is the most gigantic crime of this or any other age. The consummation of such a scheme would ultimately entail more misery upon the human race than all the wars, pestilences, and famines that ever occurred in the history of the world.

The absolute and instantaneous destruction of half the entire movable property of the world, including houses, ships, railroads, and other appliances for carrying on commerce, while it would be felt more sensibly at the moment, would not produce anything like the prolonged distress and disorganization of society that must inevitably result from the permanent annihilation of one-half the metallic money of the world.

The junior Senator from Texas (Mr. Mills) never did the party greater service than when, on the 3rd of February, 1886, on this floor he denounced, in language, the force and earnestness of which can not be surpassed, the attempted crime against silver. Let his words be an inspiration now:

But in all the wild, reckless, and remorseless brutalities that have marked the footprints of resistless power there is some extenuating circumstance that mitigates the severity of the punishment due the crime. Some have been the product of the fierce passions of war, some have come from the antipathy that separates alien races, some from the superstitions of opposing religions.

But the crime that is now sought to be perpetrated on more than fifty millions of people comes neither from the camp of a conqueror, the hand of a foreigner, nor the altar of an idolator. But it comes from those in whose veins runs the blood of the common ancestry, who were born under the same skies, speak the same language, reared in the same institutions, and nurtured in the principles of the same religious faith. It comes from the cold, phlegmatic, marble heart of avarice—avarice that seeks to paralyze labor, increase the burden of debt, and fill the land with destitution and suffering to gratify the lust for gold—avarice surrounded by every comfort that wealth can command, and rich enough to satisfy every want save that which refuses to be satisfied without the suffocation and strangulation of all the labor of the land. With a forehead that refuses to be ashamed it demands of Congress an act that will paralyze all the forces of production, shut out labor from all employment, increase the burden of debts and taxation, and send desolation and suffering to all the homes of the poor.

Can language be stronger or conclusion more conclusive? What expression can be more forcible than the "most gigantic crime of this or any other age?" What picture more vivid than that painted in the words, "The consummation of such a scheme would ultimately entail more misery upon the human race than all the wars, pestilences, and famines that ever occurred in the history of the world?" What more scathing rebuke could be administered to avarice than that contained in the words of Mr. Mills?

It is from the awful horrors described by these distinguished men, differing in politics, but united in sentiment, that I beg you, sirs, to save your fellow-men.

On the base of the monument erected by a grateful people to the memory of the late Senator Hill, of Georgia, are inscribed these words:

Who saves his country saves himself, and all things saved do bless him. Who lets his country die lets all things die, dies himself ignobly, and all things dying, curse him.

If, sirs, in saving your country you save yourselves and earn the benedictions of all things saved, how much greater will be your reward if your efforts save not your country only but all mankind! If he who lets his country die, brings upon himself the curses of all things dying; in what language will an indignant people express their execration, if your action lead to the enslavement of the great majority of the people by the universal adoption of an appreciating standard!

Let me call your attention briefly to the advantages of bimetallism. It is not claimed that by the use of two metals at a fixed ratio absolute stability can be secured. We only contend that thus the monetary unit will become more stable in relation to other property than under a single standard. If a single standard were really more desirable than a double standard, we are not free to choose gold, and would be compelled to select silver. Gold and silver must remain component parts of the metallic money of the world—that must be accepted as an indisputable fact. Our abandonment of silver would in all probability drive it out of use as primary money; and silver as a promise to pay gold is little, if any, better than a paper promise to pay. If bimetallism is impossible, then we must make up our minds to a silver standard or to the abandonment of both gold and silver.

Let us suppose the worst that has been prophesied by our opponents, namely, that we would be upon a silver standard if we attempted the free coinage of both gold and silver at any ratio. Let us suppose that all our gold goes to Europe and we have only silver. Silver would not be inconvenient to use, because a silver certificate is just as convenient to handle as a gold certificate, and the silver itself need not be handled except where it is necessary for change. Gold is not handled among the people. No one desires to accept any large amount in gold. The fact that the Treasury has always on hand a large amount of gold coin deposited in exchange for gold certificates shows that the paper representative is more desirable than the metal itself. If, following out the supposition, our gold goes abroad, Europe will have more money with which to buy our exports—cotton and wheat, cattle and hogs.

If, on the other hand, we adopt gold, we must draw it from Europe, and thus lessen their money and reduce the price of our exports in foreign markets. This, too, would decrease the total value of our exports and increase the amount of products which it would be necessary to send abroad to pay the principal and interest which we owe to bondholders and stockholders residing in Europe. Some have suggested the advisability of issuing gold bonds in order to maintain a gold standard. Let them remember that those bonds sold in this country will draw money from circulation and increase the stringency, and sold abroad will affect injuriously the price of our products abroad, thus making a double tax upon the toilers of the United States, who must ultimately pay them.

Let them remember, too, that gold bonds held abroad must some time be paid in gold, and the exportation of that gold would probably raise a clamor for an extension of time in order to save this country from another stringency. A silver standard, too, would make us the trading center of all the silver-using countries of the world, and these countries contain far more than one-half of the world's population. What in impetus would be given to our Western and Southern seaports, such as San Francisco, Galveston, New Orleans, Mobile, Savannah, and Charleston! Then, again, we produce our silver, and produce it in quantities which would to some extent satisfy our monetary needs.

On motion of Mr. Hunter the time of Mr. Bryan was extended indefinitely.

Mr. Bryan. I thank the gentleman from Illinois and the House.

Our annual product of gold is less than 50 cents per capita. Deduct from this sum the loss which would be occasioned to the gold supply by the closing of our silver mines, which produce gold in conjunction with silver; deduct, also, the amount consumed in the arts, and the amount left for coinage is really inconsiderable. Thus, with a gold standard, we would be left dependent upon foreign powers for our annual money supply. They say we must adopt a gold standard in order to trade with Europe. Why not reverse the proposition and say that Europe must resume the use of silver in order to trade with us? But why adopt either gold or silver alone? Why not adopt both and trade with both gold-using and silver-using countries? The principle of bimetallism is established upon a scientific basis.

The Government does not try to fix the purchasing power of the dollar, either gold or silver. It simply says, in the language of Thomas Jefferson, "The money unit shall stand upon the two metals," and then allows the exchangeable value of that unit to rise or fall according as the total product of both metals decreases or increases in proportion to the demand for money. In attempting to maintain the parity between the two metals at a fixed ratio, the Government does not undertake the impossible. France for several years did maintain the parity approximately at 15½ to 1, by offering unlimited coinage to both metals at that ratio. It is very common for some people to urge, "You cannot put value into anything by law," and I am sorry to see some proclaim this who know by rich experience how easy it is for the Government to legislate prices up or down.

We were called together to relieve financial distress by legislation. Some propose to relieve the present stringency of the money market by removing the tax on national bank circulation and allowing banks to issue 100 per cent. on their bonds instead of 90 per cent. This legislation would put value into bank stocks by law, because it would add to the profits of the bank, and such a law would probably raise the market price of bonds by increasing the demand for them. I will not discuss the merits of this proposition now. Let those who favor it prepare to justify themselves before their constituents. The New York World of August 3 contained an article encouraging the banks to issue more money under the present law. It showed the profits as follows:

These bonds are selling now at 109 to 110. At this latter period a $100,000 bond transaction would stand as follows:

$100,000 U. S. 4's at 110, less 1-3 per cent. accrued interest, $109,666 net, would cost ...

$109,666

Less circulation issued on this amount ...

90,000

Making the actual cash investment only ...

$19,666

On which the bank would receive an income of over 12 7/8 per cent., as follows:

Interest on $100,000 4's per annum ...

$4,000

Less tax 1 per cent. on circulation ...

$900

Less sinking fund to retire premium to be improved at 6 per cent. ...

464

Less expenses ...

100

1,464

Net income ...

$2,536

Already a good portion of these bonds held in reserve are coming into the market and will soon find their way into the hands of national banks.

If the proposed law is adopted $900 will be taken from the expense column by the repeal of the tax on circulation and $10,000 will be taken from the cost of investment, so that the profits would amount to $3,436 on an investment of $9,666, or more than 33 per cent. If, however, the increased demand for bonds raised the premium to 15 per cent., we could only calculate a little less than $3,436 on an investment of $14,666, or nearly 25 per cent. This they would probably call a fair divide. The bondholder would receive an advantage in the increased premium of, say, $25,000,000, and the national bank would be able to make about double on its investment what it does now. If the premium should increase more than 5 per cent. the bondholder would make more and the bank less. If the premium should not increase that much the bondholder would make less and the bank more. Let those, I repeat, who favor this plan, be prepared to defend it before a constituency composed of people who are not making 5 per cent. on an average on the money invested in farms or enterprises, and let those who will profit by the law cease to deny the ability of Government to increase the price of property by law. One is almost moved to tears by the sight of New England manufacturers protesting with indignation against the wisdom or possibility of giving fictitious value to a product, when for the last thirty years they have drained the rest of the country and secured artificial prices by protective tariff laws. Some of our eastern friends accuse the advocates of free coinage of favoring repudiation.

Repudiation has not been practiced much in recent years by the debtor, but in 1869 the Credit Strengthening Act enabled the bondholder to repudiate a contract made with the Government and to demand coin in payment of a bond for which he had given paper and which was payable in lawful money. That act increasing the market value of the bonds gave a profit to many who now join the beneficiaries of the act assuming the District debt in vociferous proclamation that "the Government cannot create value." Does not the location of a public building add to the value of adjacent real estate? Do not towns contest the location of a county seat because of the advantage it brings? Does not the use of gold and silver as money increase the value of each ounce of each metal?

These are called precious metals because the production is limited and cannot be increased indefinitely at will. If this Government or a number of governments can offer a market unlimited as compared with the supply, the bullion value of gold and silver can be maintained at the legal ratio. The moment one metal tends to cheapen, the use falls on it and increases its price, while the decreased demand for the dearer metal retards its rise and thus the bullion values are kept near to their legal ratio, so near that the variation can cause far less inconvenience and injustice than the variation in the exchangeable value of the unit would inflict under a single standard. The option is always given to the debtor in a double standard.

In fact, the system could not exist if the option remained with the creditor, for he would demand the dearer metal and thus increase any fluctuation in bullion values, while the option in the hands of the debtor reduces the fluctuation to the minimum. That the unit under a double standard is more stable in its relation to all other things is admitted by Jevons and proven by several illustrations. Mr. Giffen tries to avoid the force of the admission by saying that the difference in favor of the double standard is only in the proportion of 2 to 1, and therefore not sufficient to justify its adoption. It would seem that where stability is so important—and it never was so important as today, when so many long-time contracts are executed—even a slight difference in favor of the double standard ought to make it acceptable.

We established a bimetallic standard in 1792, but silver, being overvalued by our ratio of 15 to 1, stayed with us and gold went abroad, where mint ratios were more favorable.

I have here a silver coin which came from the mint in 1795. It has upon the edge these significant words: "Hundred Cents—One Dollar or Unit." It would seem, therefore, that the weight of the gold dollar was regulated by the silver dollar, and the gold pieces provided for made multiples of it. In 1834 and in 1837 the alloy was changed and the gold dollar reduced in size in order to correspond to the newly established ratio of 16 to 1. The amount of pure silver in the standard dollar has never been changed since its adoption in 1792.

The ratio of 16 to 1 overvalued gold and our silver went abroad. The silver dollar was worth about 3 cents more than the gold dollar, because it could be coined in France at the ratio of 15½ to 1. Thus during all the period prior to 1873 this country enjoyed bimetallism and, although at one time we used one metal and at another time another, no statesman arose to demand a single standard. We now have three kinds of bimetallists—those who favor a double standard only by international agreement, those who favor independent action at a changed ratio, and those who favor independent action at the present ratio. Those favoring an international agreement might be again divided into those who favor an agreement by a few nations, those who favor an agreement by many nations, and those who favor it only on condition that all nations would join.

I suppose it would hardly be proper to further divide them into those who really desire an international agreement and those who utilize the possibility of an international agreement to prevent independent action. I am afraid the agreement will not be brought about by those who, like the gentleman from Ohio (Mr. Harter), are willing to try it, but have no faith in its permanency; nor will it receive much aid, I fear, from the gentleman from New York (Mr. Hendrix), who said on last Saturday:

I predict to you that inside of three months—before this Congress meets again—if you repeal this Sherman law and adjourn, England will make proposals to ths country to come into a monetary conference and see what can be done for the sake of her ward, India.

Less than five minutes before he had pierced the veil of the future with prophetic ken and declared:

The moving finger of Time, down from the days when gold started in the race for first place to this moment, has pointed to a single unit of value. It is our destiny. It will triumph in this Hall—perhaps not in this Congress nor in your day; but it is going to become the financial policy of this country just as sure as tomorrow morning's sun will rise.

Any hope of bimetallism there?

What is the prospect for the establishment of international bimetallism? I would be glad to see the unlimited coinage of gold and silver at a fixed ratio among the nations, but how is such an agreement to be secured? The gentleman from Maryland (Mr. Rayner) says the unconditional repeal of the Sherman law will bring England to terms. Is it impossible to extract a lion's teeth without putting your head in his mouth? Is it not a dangerous experiment to join England in a single standard in order to induce her to join us in a double standard? International agreement is an old delusion and has done important duty on many previous occasions.

The opponents of the Bland law in 1878 were waiting for international bimetallism. Mr. Cleveland mentioned the prospect of it in his message in 1885, and again this year. It was a valuable weapon in 1890, when the Sherman bill was passed and the Brussels conference was called in time to carry us over the last Presidential election. We are still waiting, and those are waiting most patiently who favor a gold standard. Are we any nearer to an international agreement than we were fifteen years ago? The European nations wait on England, and she refused within a year to even consider the adoption of the double standard. Can we conquer her by waiting? We have tried the Fabian policy.

Suppose we try bringing her to terms by action. Let me appeal to your patriotism. Shall we make our laws dependent upon England's action and thus allow her to legislate for us upon the most important of all questions? Shall we confess our inability to enact monetary laws? Are we an English colony or an independent people? If the use of gold alone is to make us slaves, let us use both metals and be free. If there be some living along the eastern coast—better acquainted with the beauties of the Alps than with the grandeur of the Rockies, more accustomed to the sunny skies of Italy than to the invigorating breezes of the Mississippi Valley—who are not willing to trust their fortunes and their destinies to American citizens, let them learn that the people living between the Alleghanies to the Golden Gate are not afraid to cast their all upon the Republic and rise or fall with it.

One hundred and seventeen years ago the liberty bell gave notice to a waiting and expectant people that independence had been declared. There may be doubting, trembling ones among us now, but, sirs, I do not overestimate it when I say that out of twelve millions of voters, more than ten millions are waiting, anxiously waiting, for the signal which shall announce the financial independence of the United States. This Congress cannot more surely win the approval of a grateful people than by declaring that this nation, the grandest which the world has ever seen, has the right and the ability to legislate for its own people on every subject, regardless of the wishes, the entreaties, or the threats of foreign powers.

Perhaps the most important question for us to consider is the question of ratio. Comparatively few people in this country are in favor of a gold standard, and no national party has ever advocated it. Comparatively few, also, will be deceived by the promise of international bimetallism annually held out to us. Among those in favor of bimetallism, and in favor of independent action on the part of the United States, there is, however, an honest difference of opinion as to the particular ratio at which the unlimited coinage of gold and silver should be undertaken. The principle of bimetallism does not stand upon any certain ratio, and may exist at 1 to 30 as well as at 1 to 16.

In fixing the ratio we should select that one which will secure the greatest advantage to the public and cause the least injustice. The present ratio, in my judgment, should be adopted. A change in the ratio could be made (as in 1834) by reducing the size of the gold dollar or by increasing the size of the silver dollar, or by making a change in the weight of both dollars. A large silver dollar would help the creditor. A smaller gold dollar would help the debtor. It is not just to do either, but if a change must be made the benefit should be given to the debtor rather than to the creditor.

Let no one accuse me of defending the justness of any change; but I repeat it, if we are given a choice between a change which will aid the debtor by reducing the size of his debt and a change which will aid the creditor by increasing the amount which he is to receive, either by increasing the number of his dollars or their size, the advantage must be given to the debtor, and no man during this debate, whatever may be his private wish or interest, will advocate the giving of the advantage to the creditor.

To illustrate the effect of changing the ratio let us take, for convenience, the ratio of 24 to 1, as advocated by some. We could make this change by reducing the weight of the gold dollar one-third. This would give to the holders of gold an advantage of some $200,000,000, but the creditors would lose several billions of dollars in the actual value of their debts. A debt contracted before 1873 would not be scaled, because the new gold dollar would purchase as much as the old gold dollar would in 1873. Creditors, however, whose loans have been made since that time would suffer, and the most recent loans would show the greatest loss. The value of silver bullion has only fallen in relation to gold. But the purchasing power of one ounce of silver has varied less since 1873 than has the purchasing power of one ounce of gold, which would indicate that gold had risen.

If, on the other hand, the ratio is changed by increasing the size of the silver dollar, it would be necessary to recoin our silver dollars into dollars a half larger, or we would have in circulation two legal tender silver dollars of different sizes. Of the two plans it would be better, in my judgment, to keep both dollars in circulation together, though unequal in weight, rather than to recoin the lighter dollars. The recoinage of more than 500,000,000 of silver dollars, or the bullion representing them, would cause a shrinkage of about $170,000,000, or one-third of our silver money; it would cause a shrinkage of nearly one-sixth of our metallic money and of more than one-tenth of our total circulation. This contraction would increase our debts more than a billion dollars and decrease the nominal value of our property more than five billions.

A change in the ratio made by increasing the size of the silver dollar as above suggested would also decrease by one-third the number of dollars which could be coined from the annual product of silver. If, as Mr. Carlisle has said, the supply of metal, both gold and silver, is none too large to keep pace with population, the increase in the weight of each dollar would make the supply to that extent deficient. A change in ratio, whether secured by decreasing the gold dollar or by increasing the silver dollar, would probably make an international agreement more difficult, because nearly all of the silver coin now in existence circulates at a ratio less than ours.

If the change should be made in this country by increasing the size of the silver dollar and an international agreement secured upon the new ratio, to be effected by other nations in the same way, the amount of money in the world, that is metallic money, would suffer a contraction of more than $1,000,000,000, to the enormous injury of the debtor class and to the enormous advantage of the creditor class. If we believe that the value of gold has risen because its supply has not increased as fast as the demand caused by favorable legislation, then it would be unfair to continue this appreciation by other legislation favorable to gold. It would be a special injustice to the mine owner and to the farmer, whose products have fallen with silver, to make perpetual the injunction against their prosperity.

We often hear our opponents complain of the "cupidity of the mine owner." Let us admit that the mine owner is selfish, and that he will profit by the increased price of silver bullion. Let us, for the sake of argument, go further, and accuse him of favoring the free coinage of silver solely for the purpose of increasing the price of his product. Does that make him worse than other men? Is not the farmer selfish enough to desire a higher price for wheat? Is not the cotton-grower selfish enough to desire a higher price for his cotton? Is not the laboring man selfish enough to desire higher wages? And, if I may be pardoned for the boldness, are not bankers and business men selfish enough to ask for legislation at our hands which will give them prosperity? Was not this extraordinary session called in order to bring back prosperity to our business men?

Is it any more important that you should keep a mercantile house from failing than that you should keep a mine from suspending? Are those who desire free coinage of silver in order that the barren wastes should be made to "blossom like the rose" any worse than those who want the Sherman law repealed in order to borrow foreign gold and retire clearing house certificates? There is a class of people whose interest in financial legislation is too often overlooked. The money-loaner has just as much interest in the rise in the value of his product—money—as farmers and miners have in the increased price of their products.

The man who has $10,000 in money becomes worth $20,000 in reality when prices fall one-half. Shall we assume that the money-lenders of this and other countries ignore the advantage which an appreciated currency gives to them and desire it simply for the benefit of the poor man and the laborer? What refining influence is there in their business which purges away the dross of selfishness and makes pure and patriotic only their motives? Has some new dispensation reversed the parable and left Lazarus in torment while Dives is borne aloft in Abraham's bosom?

But is the silver miner after all so selfish as to be worthy of censure? Does he ask for some new legislation or for some innovation inaugurated in his behalf? No. He pleads only for the restoration of the money of the fathers. He asks to have given back to him a right which he enjoyed from 1792 to 1873. During all those years he could deposit his silver bullion at the mints and receive full legal tender coins at the rate of $1.29 for each ounce of silver, and during a part of the time his product could be converted into money at even a higher price. Free coinage can only give back to him what demonetization took away. He does not ask for a silver dollar redeemable in a gold dollar, but for a silver dollar which redeems itself.

If the bullion value of silver has not been reduced by hostile legislation, the free coinage of silver at the present ratio can bring to the mine owner no benefit, except by enabling him to pay a debt already contracted with less ounces of silver. If the price of his product has been reduced by hostile legislation, is he asking any more than we would ask under the same circumstances in seeking to remove the oppressive hand of the law? Let me suggest, too, that those who favor an international agreement are estopped from objecting to the profits of the silver mine owner, because an international agreement could only be effected at some ratio near to ours, probably 15½ to 1, and this would just as surely inure to the benefit of the owner of silver as would free coinage established by the independent action of this country.

If our opponents were correct in asserting that the price of silver bullion could be maintained at 129 cents an ounce by international agreement, but not by our separate action, then international bimetallism would bring a larger profit to the mine owner than the free coinage of silver by this country could. Let the international bimetallist, then, find some better objection to free coinage than that based on the mine owner's profit.

But what is the mine owner's profit? Has anyone told you the average cost of mining an ounce of silver? You have heard of some particular mine where silver can be produced at a low cost, but no one has attempted to give you any reliable data as to the average cost of production. I had a letter from Mr. Leech when he was Director of the Mint, saying that the Government is in possession of no data in regard to the cost of gold production and none of any value in regard to silver. No calculation can be made as to the profits of mining which does not include money spent in prospecting and in mines which have ceased to pay, as well as those which are profitably worked.

When we see a wheel of fortune with twenty-four paddles, see those paddles sold for 10 cents apiece, and see the holder of the winning paddle draw $2, we do not conclude that money can be profitably invested in a wheel of fortune. We know that those who bought expended altogether $2.40 on the turn of the wheel, and that the man who won only received $2; but our opponents insist upon estimating the profits of silver mining by the cost of the winning paddle. It is safe to say that taking the gold and silver of the world—and it is more true of silver than of gold—every dollar's worth of metal has cost a dollar. It is strange that those who watch so carefully lest the silver miner shall receive more for his product than the bare cost of production ignore the more fortunate gold miner.

Did you ever hear a monometallist complain because a man could produce 25.8 grains of gold, 9 fine, at any price whatever, and yet take it to our mint and have it stamped into a dollar with full legal tender qualities? I saw at the World's Fair a few days ago a nugget of gold, just as it was found, worth over $3,000. What an outrage that the finder should be allowed to convert that into money at such an enormous profit! And yet no advocate of honest money raises his hand to stop that crime.

The fact is that the price of gold and silver does not depend upon the cost of production, but upon the law of supply and demand. It is true that production will stop when either metal cannot be produced at a profit; but so long as the demand continues equal to the supply the value of an ounce of either metal may be far above the cost of production. With most kinds of property a rise in price will cause increased production; for instance, if the price of wheat rises faster than the price of other things, there will be a tendency to increased production until the price falls; but this tendency cannot be carried out in the case of the precious metals, because the metals must be found before it can be produced, and finding is uncertain.

Between 1800 and 1849 an ounce of gold or silver would exchange for more of other things than it would from 1849 to 1873, yet during the latter period the production of both gold and silver greatly increased. It will be said that the purchasing power of an ounce of metal fell because of the increased supply; but that fall did not check production, nor has the rise in the purchasing power of an ounce of gold since 1873 increased the production. The production of both gold and silver is controlled so largely by chance as to make some of the laws applicable to other property inapplicable to the precious metals. If the supply of gold decreases without any diminution of the demand the exchangeable value of each ounce of gold is bound to increase, although the cost of producing the gold may continue to fall.

Why do not the advocates of gold monometallism recognize and complain of the advantage given to gold by laws which increase the demand for it and, therefore, the value of each ounce? Instead of that they confine themselves to the denunciation of the silver-mine owner. I have never advocated the use of either gold or silver as the means of giving employment to miners, nor has the defence of bimetallism been conducted by those interested in the production of silver. We favor the use of gold and silver as money because money is a necessity and because these metals, owing to special fitness, have been used from time immemorial. The entire annual supply of both metals, coined at the present ratio, does not afford too large a sum of money.

If, as is estimated, two-thirds of the $130,000,000 of gold produced annually are consumed in the arts, only $46,000,000—or less than we need for this country alone—are left to coinage. If one-sixth of the $185,000,000 of silver produced annually is used in the arts, $155,000,000 are left for coinage. India has been in the habit of taking about one-third of that sum. Thus the total amount of gold and silver annually available for all the people of all the world is only about $200,000,000, or about four times what we need in this country to keep pace with increasing population. And as population increases the annual addition to the money must also increase.

The total sum of metallic money is a little less than $8,000,000,000. The $200,000,000 per annum is about two-and-a-half per cent. on the total volume of metallic money, taking no account of lost coins and shrinkage by abrasion. To quote again the language of Mr. Carlisle.

Mankind will be fortunate indeed if the annual production of gold coin shall keep pace with the annual increase of population, commerce and industry.

An increase of the silver dollar one-third by an international agreement would reduce by 50,000,000 the number of dollars which could be coined from the annual product of silver, which would amount to a decrease of about one-fourth of the entire increase of metallic money, while the abandonment of silver entirely would destroy three-quarters of the annual increase in metallic money, or possibly all of it, if we take into consideration the reduction of the gold supply by the closing of gold-producing silver mines.

Thus it is almost certain that without silver the sum of metallic money would remain stationary, if not actually decrease, from year to year, while population increases and new enterprises demand, from time to time, a larger sum of currency. Thus it will be seen that the money question is broader than the interest of a few mine owners. It touches every man, woman, and child in all the world, and affects those in every condition of life and society.

The interest of the mine owner is incidental. He profits by the use of silver as money just as the gold miner profits by the use of gold as money; just as the newspaper profits by the law compelling the advertising of foreclosures; just as the seaport profits by the deepening of its harbor; just as the horse seller would profit by a war which required the purchase of a large number of horses for cavalry service, or just as the undertaker would profit by the decent burial of a pauper at public expense.

All of these receive an incidental benefit from public acts. Shall we complain if the use of gold and silver as money gives employment to men, builds up cities and fills our mountains with life and industry? Shall we oppress all debtors and derange all business agreements in order to prevent the producers of money metals from obtaining for them more than actual cost? We do not reason that way in other things; why suppress the reason in this matter because of cultivated prejudices against the white metal? But what interest has the farmer in this subject, you may ask. The same that every laboring man has in a currency sufficient to carry on the commerce and business of a country. The employer cannot give work to men unless he can carry on the business at a profit, and he is hampered and embarrassed by a currency which appreciates because of its insufficiency.

The farmer labors under a double disadvantage. He not only suffers as a producer from all those causes which reduce the price of property, but he is thrown into competition with the products of India. Without Indian competition his lot would be hard enough, for if he is a land owner he finds his capital decreasing with an appreciating standard, and if he owes on the land he finds his equity of redemption extinguished. The last census shows a real estate mortgage indebtedness in the five great agricultural States— Illinois, Iowa, Missouri, Kansas and Nebraska—of more than one billion of dollars. A rising standard means a great deal of distress to these mortgagors. But as I said, the producers of wheat and cotton have a special grievance, for the prices of those articles are governed largely by the prices in Liverpool, and as silver goes down our prices fall, while the rupee price remains the same. I quote from the agricultural report of 1890, page 8:

The recent legislation looking to the restoration of the bimetallic standard of our currency, and the consequent enhancement of the value of silver, has unquestionably had much to do with the recent advance in the price of cereals. The same cause has advanced the price of wheat in Russia and India, and in the same degree reduced their power of competition. English gold was formerly exchanged for cheap silver and wheat purchased with the cheaper metal was sold in Great Britain for gold. Much of this advantage is lost by the appreciation of silver in those countries. It is reasonable, therefore, to expect much higher prices for wheat than have been received in recent years.

Mr. Rusk's reasoning is correct. Shall we by changing the ratio fix the price of wheat and cotton at the present low price? If it is possible to do so it is no more than fair that we restore silver to its former place, and thus give back to the farmer some of his lost prosperity. Can silver be maintained on a parity with gold at the present ratio? It has been shown that if we should fail and our effort should result in a single silver standard it would be better for us than the adoption of the gold standard—that is, that the worst that could come from the attempt would be far better than the best that our opponents could offer us.

It has been shown that dangers and disadvantages attend a change of ratio. It may now be added that no change in the ratio can be made with fairness or intelligence without first putting gold and silver upon a perfect equality in order to tell what the natural ratio is. If a new ratio is necessary, who can tell just what that ratio ought to be? Who knows to what extent the divergence between gold and silver is due to natural laws and to what extent it is due to artificial laws? We know that the mere act of India in suspending free coinage, although she continues to buy and coin on government account, reduced the price of silver more than 10 cents per ounce. Can anyone doubt that the restoration of free coinage in that country would increase the bullion price of silver? Who doubts that the free coinage of silver by the United States would increase its bullion price?

The only question is how much. Is it only a guess, for no one can state with mathematical precision what the rise would be. The full use of silver, too, would stop the increased demand for gold, and thus prevent any further rise in its price. It is because no one can speak with certainty that I insist that no change in the ratio can be intelligently made until both metals are offered equal privileges at the mint. When we have the free and unlimited coinage of gold and silver at the present ratio, then, and then only, can we tell whether any of the apparent fall in the bullion price of silver is due to circumstances over which we have no control, if so, how much? If this experiment should demonstrate the necessity for a change of ratio it can be easily made, and should be made in such a way as to cause the least injury to society. But we can, in my judgment, maintain the parity at the present ratio. I state this without hesitation, notwithstanding the fact that our opponents do not disguise the contempt which they feel for one who can believe this possible. If the past teaches anything it teaches the possibility of this country maintaining the parity alone. The Royal Commission of England stated in its report that France did maintain the parity at 15½ to 1, although she has not half our population or enterprise. During the years when her mint laws controlled the price of gold and silver bullion the changes in the relative production of gold and silver were greater than they have been since. At one time before 1873 the value of the silver product was related to the value of the gold product as 3 to 1, while at another time the relation was reversed, and the production of gold to silver was as 3 to 1.

No such changes have occurred since; and the present value of the silver product is only 1½ to 1 of gold. Much of the prejudice against silver is due to the fact that it has been falling as compared to gold. Let it begin to rise and it will become more acceptable as a money metal. Goschen, at the Paris Conference, very aptly stated the condition when he said:

At present there is a vicious circle. States are afraid of employing silver on account of the depreciation, and the depreciation continues because States refuse to employ it.

Let that "vicious circle" be broken and silver will resume its rightful place. We believe, in other words, that the opening of our mints to the free and unlimited coinage of gold and silver at 16 to 1 would immediately result in restoring silver to the coinage value of $1.29 per ounce, not only here, but everywhere. That there could be no difference between the dollar coined and the same weight of silver uncoined, when one could be exchanged for the other, needs no argument.

We do not believe that the gold dollar would go to a premium, because it could not find a better coinage ratio elsewhere, and because it could be put to no purpose for which a silver dollar would not be as good. If our ratio were 1 to 14 our gold would of course be exchanged for silver; but with our ratio of 16 to 1 gold is worth more here than abroad, and foreign silver would not come here, because it is circulating at home at a better ratio than we offer.

We need not concern ourselves, therefore, about the coin silver. All that we have to take care of is the annual product from the mines, about 40 per cent. of which is produced in this country. Under the Sherman law we furnish a market for about one-third of the world's annual product. I believe about one-sixth is used in the arts, which would leave about one-half for all the rest of the world. India has suspended free coinage temporarily, in anticipation of the repeal of the Sherman law. The Herschell report expressly states that the action was necessary, because no agreement with the United States could be secured. The language is as follows:

In a dispatch of the 30th of June, 1892, the government of India expressed the deliberate opinion that, if it became clear that the Brussels conference was unlikely to arrive at a saisfactory conclusion, and if a direct agreement between India and the United States were found to be unattainable, the government of India should at once close their mints to the free coinage of silver and make arrangements for the introduction of the gold standard.

There is no doubt of the restoration of free coinage in India if this Government takes the lead, and with India taking the usual amount, but one-sixth of the annual supply is left for the other silver-using countries. There can be no flood of silver, nor will prices rise to any considerable extent—except the price of silver itself and a few of the staple products of agriculture which have fallen with silver because of India's competition. General prices cannot rise unless the total number of dollars increases more rapidly than the need for dollars, which has been shown to be impossible. The danger is, that taking all the gold and all the silver, we will not have enough money, and that there will still be some appreciation in the standard of value.

To recapitulate, then, there is not enough of either metal to form the basis for the world's metallic money; both metals must therefore be used as full legal tender primary money. There is not enough of both metals to more than keep pace with the increased demand for money; silver cannot be retained in circulation as a part of the world's money if the United States abandons it. This nation must, therefore, either retain the present law or make some further provision for silver. The only rational plan is to use both gold and silver at some ratio with equal privileges at the Mint. No change in the ratio can be made intelligently until both metals are put on an equality at the present ratio. The present ratio should be adopted if the parity can be maintained; and, lastly, it can be.

If these conclusions are correct what must be our action on the bill to unconditionally repeal the Sherman law? The Sherman law has a serious defect; it treats silver as a commodity rather than as a money, and thus discriminates between silver and gold. The Sherman law was passed in 1890 as a substitute for what was known as the Bland law. It will be remembered that the Bland law was forced upon the silver men as a compromise, and that the opponents of silver sought its repeal from the day it was passed. It will also be remembered that the Sherman law was in like manner forced upon the silver men as a compromise, and that the opponents of silver have sought its repeal ever since it became a law. The law provides for the compulsory purchase of 54,000,000 ounces of silver per year, and for the issue of Treasury notes thereon at the gold value of the bullion.

These notes are a legal tender and are redeemable in gold or silver at the option of the Government. There is also a clause in the law which states that it is the policy of this Government to maintain the parity between the metals. The Administration, it seems, has decided that the parity can only be maintained by violating a part of the law and giving the option to the holder instead of to the Government. Without discussing the administration of the law let us consider the charges made against it.

The main objection which we heard last spring was that the Treasury notes were used to draw gold out of the Treasury. If that objection were a material one the bill might easily be amended so as to make the Treasury notes hereafter issued redeemable only in silver, like the silver certificates issued under the Bland law. But the objection is scarcely important enough for consideration. While the Treasury notes have been used to draw out gold, they need not have been used for that purpose, for we have $346,000,000 worth of greenbacks with which gold can be drawn, so long as the Government gives the option to the holder. If all of the Treasury notes were destroyed the greenbacks are sufficient to draw out the $100,000,000 reserve three times over, and then they can be reissued and used again. To complain of the Treasury notes while the greenbacks remain is like finding fault because the gate is open when the whole fence is down, and reminds me of the man who made a box for his feline family, and cut a big hole for the cat to go in at and a little hole for the kittens to go in at, forgetting that the large hole would do for cats of all sizes.

Just at this time the law is being made the scapegoat upon which all our financial ills are loaded, and its immediate and unconditional repeal is demanded as the sole means by which prosperity can be restored to a troubled people.

The main accusation against it now is that it destroys confidence and that foreign money will not come here, because the holder is afraid that we will go to a silver standard. The exportation of gold has been pointed to as conclusive evidence that frightened English bondholders were throwing American securities upon the market and selling them to our people in exchange for gold. But now gold is coming back faster than it went away, and still we have the Sherman law unrepealed. Since that theory will not explain both the export and import of gold, let us accept a theory which will. The balance of trade has been largely against us during the last year, and gold went abroad to pay it, but now our exportation of breadstuffs has increased and the gold is returning. Its going was aggravated by the fact that Austria-Hungary was gathering in gold for resumption and was compelled to take a part from us. Instead of using that export of gold as a reason for going to a gold basis, it ought to make us realize the danger of depending solely upon a metal which some other nation may deprive us of at a critical moment.

...

Source: William J. Bryan, The First Battle: A Story of the Campaign of 1896 (Chicago: W. B. Conkey Company, 1896), pp. 77-114.

Commenting on this speech (see Chapter 2), Bryan writes:

From what had already taken place I felt sure that the great contest over the money question was approaching and after the adjournment of Congress devoted myself to preparation for it. I was not surprised, therefore, when the President called Congress together in extraordinary session on the 7th day of August, 1893. Mr. Wilson of West Virginia, chairman of the

Committee of Ways and Means, introduced the Administration measure, to which I have heretofore referred, and the great parliamentary struggle began. I then asserted, and still believe, that the debate over the repeal bill was the most important economic discussion which ever took place in our Congress. On the 16th day of August, 1893, near the close of the debate, I delivered in opposition to unconditional repeal. The bill passed the House by a considerable majority and after nearly two months of debate in the Senate, came back to the House with an amendment.

www.ingramcontent.com/pod-product-compliance
Lightning Source LLC
Chambersburg PA
CBHW060350290526
45791CB00004B/1608